Published by Creative Education

P.O. Box 227, Mankato, Minnesota 56002

Creative Education is an imprint of The Creative Company.

Design and production by Stephanie Blumenthal

Printed in the United States of America

Photographs by Alamy (Lebrecht Music & Art, Jamie Marshall, Mary Evans Picture Library,

Popperfoto), Corbis (Alinari Archives, Asian Art & Archaeology, Bettman, Burstein Collection,

Christie's Images, Werner Forman, Peter Harholdt, Michael Maslan Historic Photographs,

Rykoff, Stapleton Collection, Keren Su), Getty Images (Al Freni)

Library of Congress Cataloging-in-Publication Data

Hanel, Rachael.

Samurai / by Rachael Hanel.

p. cm. — (Fearsome fighters)

Includes bibliographical references and index.

ISBN-13: 978-1-58341-538-2

1. Samurai—Juvenile literature. I. Title.

DS827.S3H36 2007

355.00952—dc22   2006023575

First edition

2 4 6 8 9 7 5 3 1

SAMURAI

RACHAEL HANEL

FEARSOME FIGHTERS

CREATIVE EDUCATION

778.

From the beginning of time, wherever groups of people have lived together, they have also fought among themselves. Some have fought for control of basic necessities—food, water, and shelter—or territory. Others have been spurred to fight by religious differences. Still others have fought solely for sport. Throughout the ages, some fighters have taken up arms willingly; others have been forced into battle. For all, however, the ultimate goal has always been victory.

In Japan, samurai warriors fought at the command of their masters for control of land and territory. For more than 700 years, they slashed, shot, and pierced their way across battlefields. Yet, when not engaged in violent conflict, samurai led quiet, contemplative lives. They lived by a code that required extreme self-discipline and respect for others. This discipline and peace penetrated all aspects of their lives, for samurai knew that the day would come when they might be asked to die for their master. When that moment came, they wanted to face death in the same way they faced life—with calm understanding and courage. Samurai's long-lasting tenure over centuries places them among the most successful and enduring warriors the world has ever known.

THE RISE OF THE WARRIOR

Samurai began to dominate the Japanese landscape in the 12th century A.D., at a time when powerful families ruled Europe and Africa and a sophisticated culture thrived in Asia. Asian nations followed complex political systems, and religious practices such as **Shintoism, Buddhism,** and **Confucianism** dominated all ways of life. On the mainland, Asia's different cultures mixed through vast trading networks that specialized in silk and spices, and Asians exchanged goods and thoughts with Europeans and Africans. But because Japan was an island nation, it missed out on most of this trade, as contact with other nations was nearly impossible. Thus, the country remained relatively isolated from the rest of the world.

Japan did have some contact with China, however, and had since the first century A.D. Over the centuries, the Chinese had influenced Japanese culture, bringing Buddhism to the island in the sixth century A.D. A distinct Japanese culture and way of life emerged around the eighth century as the Japanese made Chinese ideas, such as Buddhism and art, their own. The Japanese ruling regime also adopted a Chinese-style political system with a strong **central government** led by an emperor. Japanese rulers were not without problems, however, and by the late 12th century, the central government was corrupt and weakened.

In 1185, a powerful military leader named Yoritomo (1147–99) forced the emperor to give him the title of shogun, or "barbarian-conquering supreme general." The shogun became the ruler of the country, while the emperor was relegated to a solely ceremonial role. Japan was then divided into a number of large estates, most of which were given tax-free to rich and powerful men known as daimyo. Power filtered down through the shogun to the daimyo,

THE BUDDHA'S TEACHINGS FORM THE BASIS OF BUDDHISM

and as peasant farmers—who now bore the brunt of the country's tax burden—struggled to eke out a living, they had no choice but to sell their land to the already rich daimyo, who gained control of larger and larger tracts of land. Each daimyo ruled over his own section of land, and as a result, order was difficult to maintain. Roving bands of rebels stirred up trouble by **ransacking** the castles of daimyo, destroying crops, conquering lands, and preying upon people traveling the country's trade routes. Eventually, daimyo turned to independent warriors for protection, and the age of the samurai was born.

Samurai—which means "one who serves"—first acted as guards for the daimyo. Violent battles between daimyo over territory were common, as land suitable for agricultural development was in short supply. Daimyo needed samurai to help them retain their lands as well as to fight to obtain new territory, and organized samurai armies soon became a necessary component of Japanese society. As their services were needed more and more, samurai's influence grew, and they soon became an important **aristocratic** class.

Despite their position of importance in Japanese society, most samurai lived simply. Their masters provided them with food and shelter, so they didn't need much money. Samurai either lived in the same castle as their daimyo or nearby in the same village. If a daimyo had much

SOME SAMURAI FOUGHT SINGLE-HANDEDLY ON FOOT (ABOVE), OTHERS ON HORSEBACK (OPPOSITE)

Although samurai are the best-known warriors from Japanese history, they were by no means the first fighters to emerge in Japan. Centuries-old accounts tell the first stories of warriors who embraced characteristics that later would become common among samurai. The Nihongi (Chronicles of Japan) *mentions the use of archers on horseback in an* A.D. 672 *battle, which possibly became an early model for samurai. Some of the earliest fighters in Japan were the Yamato people, who came to the country from the Korean peninsula around* A.D. 250. *They rode on horseback, carried steel swords, and wore iron armor. They conquered many Japanese tribes through the seventh century.*

land and therefore hundreds of samurai, the warriors might be scattered throughout his land in different castles. Occasionally, samurai became rich if their daimyo granted them a piece of land or if they married a woman from a wealthy family. In that case, they ruled over peasants, farmers, and merchants.

Daimyo often called on their samurai to spend weeks or months away from home, fighting to acquire land in faraway places. When they weren't away in battle, samurai spent time at home with their families. Samurai married, but usually not for love. Instead, marriages between samurai and women were arranged, often by a daimyo or higher-ranking samurai. The brides might be daughters of samurai. Poorer samurai did not have to marry a woman from a samurai family; they could marry common villagers. If a bride's parents were rich, they gave the samurai money so the couple could start a good life together.

Whether rich or poor, samurai sported a unique look. They draped themselves in flowing robes, called kimonos. Richer samurai wore kimonos made of silk. These robes featured neutral tones, free of outlandish colors and patterns. A samurai's wife wore the same colors as her husband. Children were allowed to wear more colorful outfits, but these grew more subdued as they reached adulthood. Elderly samurai clad themselves in grays and browns to reflect their quiet, dignified ways. Underneath their kimonos, samurai wore loose trousers. They finished the look with a jacket draped over their kimono. Samurai wore their hair in a distinctive style. They let it grow long in the back but would shave the front. Then they pulled their hair into a knot at the top of their heads. Moustaches and beards were also important, as they symbolized manhood.

The central focus of a samurai's life was the bushido code. This code—a set of **morals**—stressed loyalty to one's master, self-discipline, and living in a respectful, polite manner. A samurai lived a quiet life. He was not to argue or yell.

忠臣蔵

二伇目

A samurai gathered many names during his lifetime. At birth, he was anointed with a name that indicated good fortune. He might also be known by one of many common household nicknames. For example, the eldest son in a household was known as "Taro." At his coming-of-age ceremony, a samurai received his first adult name. These names generally were considered "gifts" from well-known and powerful people. The Japanese language revolves around characters, and receiving a character that was part of an important person's name was considered a great gift. As they grew older, samurai might change their own names to mark a particular event or to gain political favor.

SAMURAI WERE POPULAR
SUBJECTS IN JAPANESE ART

He did not drink excessive amounts of alcohol, and he treated women with respect. The bushido code also stressed the importance of education. A samurai warrior relied on more than just his physical strength. He was also to be a smart, well-rounded man, well-versed in all aspects of life. Samurai studied many different subjects, including poetry, art, dancing, and mathematics.

In whatever a samurai did—eat, fight, love, rest—the bushido code stressed that he must always think about death. Day and night, a samurai contemplated the inevitable end of his life. This preoccupation with death was meant to prepare a samurai for battle, for a samurai warrior, more than others, faced the prospect of a violent and painful death at a young age. A samurai was honored to fight courageously in battle, wanting to prove his loyalty and devotion to his

SAMURAI USED STRATEGY (ABOVE) AS WELL AS FINELY HONED PHYSICAL SKILLS (OPPOSITE) TO TRIUMPH IN BATTLE

daimyo. An even greater honor was to die on the battlefield in a fight for his master. Fighting nobly to the death—facing it calmly and without hysterics—was a respected way to meet one's end.

Because of the dignified manner in which samurai conducted themselves, they were held in high regard by the Japanese public. As samurai culture took firmer hold, the samurai's status continued to rise. Eventually, the samurai became a high, respected class—the warrior class. Only samurai were allowed to carry weapons, and they could kill anyone who disrespected them. A samurai didn't have to work; his lord asked him only to fight.

A VICIOUS WAY TO FIGHT

A samurai's weapons did not serve simply as tools to inflict injury; they were an extension of the samurai, a part of his family, a part of his soul. A samurai treated his weapons with the utmost respect. Bushido code did not allow a samurai to draw his weapon when not at war. To do so was considered rude and disrespectful, a violation of the code. No self-respecting samurai would ever misuse any of his weapons.

The sword was the samurai's most important weapon. According to legend, a samurai's spirit resided within his sword. He never let it leave his side. It was so important to him that he might even sleep with it under his pillow at night. When a samurai entered a home, bushido code demanded that he leave his weapons at the door. But he might carry a small sword at his side at all times, reluctant to become totally unarmed in case danger might arise.

Samurai weren't the only people to hold the sword in high regard. Swordsmiths, too, looked upon the weapons with respect. A swordsmith took special care when **forging** a sword, for it would contain a samurai's spirit. Before starting work, the swordsmith prayed and bathed. He clothed himself all in white and went about making swords in a quiet, respectful manner, almost like a priest. Swordsmiths relied on ancient rituals and old family techniques in their work. In order to curve a sword's blade, swordsmiths heated iron to high temperatures, then quickly dipped it into a pool of cool water, where it was bent. The best swordsmiths folded the slumped iron over and over again in the fire, creating a remarkably strong weapon.

The samurai's long, curved sword—the *katana*—developed from swords early warriors saw northern tribes use. Until then, fighters had carried a traditional straight sword. But samurai

THE KATANA WAS MORE THAN SIMPLY A USEFUL WEAPON

noticed how the curved blade inflicted deeper and more severe cuts when thrust into a man from on horseback. Samurai tended to use downward or horizontal motions when wielding their swords. A samurai also carried a smaller sword—the *wakizashi*—which was not used in fighting but instead served to cut off an opponent's head for proof of victory.

Although the sword was the samurai's favored weapon, he also used other weapons on the battlefield. Bows and arrows were used to cause injury from a long range—up to about 165 feet (50 m). Usually, samurai fired arrows from behind a big, portable **bamboo** wall at the front lines, but a skilled rider might also fire from atop his galloping horse.

The spear became a popular weapon in the 15th century as battlefield skirmishes grew more organized. Spears were often more effective than long swords against samurai who used a modified katana designed especially for riding horseback. Samurai also used a chain with heavy weights at both ends for defense against swords. Once a weapon became tangled in the chain, a samurai could easily disarm his opponent.

The *tessen* also proved to be an effective weapon. This folding iron fan could be carried discreetly in a samurai's belt; when folded, it did not take up much space. But unfolded, it could cause serious harm. The tessen was used mostly in self-defense—to knock an opponent's weapon from his hands. Rarely would a tessen alone inflict death or serious injury. In contrast, a pointed metal bar also used as a weapon could pierce through armor, quickly causing mortal wounds.

In the mid-16th century, European explorers introduced the **matchlock rifle** to Japan. Samurai adopted this weapon, which they called the *teppo*. The teppo was effective when defending a castle, as fighters could fire down upon their opponents. On the battlefield, those firing teppo positioned themselves along the front lines, near the archers. A *teppo-taisho*, or rifle commander, led teppo squadrons. The teppo-taisho tried to create a constant rate of fire, using many warriors. Opposing soldiers hid behind bales of hay or rolled bamboo to protect themselves from the flying bullets.

While the wives of samurai did not undergo formal weapons training, they sometimes were called upon to defend their homes if their husbands were away in battle. Women didn't use traditional weapons but carried a subtle emergency weapon: the hairpin. Japanese women used

MAKING A SAMURAI'S SWORD WAS A RITE OF PERFECTION

*C*reators of samurai swords took great care not only in forging the weapons, but also in making sure they were sharp and useful. A swordsmith used human bodies to test a weapon's sharpness. He made 20 cuts upon a corpse or a criminal awaiting death to see how effective the sword was, then faithfully recorded the results. He might note that a sword cut a man in half, or that one blade was able to cut off eight arms. Once the sword passed muster, it was presented to the samurai.

hairpins—some six inches (15 cm) long—to hold their long hair in place on top of their heads. In an emergency, the hairpin could be pulled out and inflict serious injury upon an enemy.

To protect himself from the onslaught of weapons attacks, a samurai dressed in an all-encompassing suit of armor that consisted of many different iron plates connected by colorful silk strings. Dressing in full battle armor was a complex and multistep process. First, the samurai donned his **breechcloth**. Then he pulled on his kimono and cinched it around his waist. From there, he stepped into loose trousers. He pulled these tight around his waist and ankles using drawstrings; his pants appeared to billow around his legs.

With his undergarments in place, the samurai was ready to put on his armor. Over the trousers, shin guards protected the samurai's lower legs. Thigh guards served the same purpose on his upper legs. He pulled metal sleeves over his arms. Then he put on the largest piece of armor, a chest plate, which went over his chest and legs. The legs piece was split so he could easily sit astride his horse. Shoulder guards went on top of

the chest plate to shield the samurai from arrows.

At each hip, the samurai tucked a sword into his belt. An iron collar protected his vulnerable throat. Before he placed his helmet on his head, he tied on a soft cotton cap and put on his face mask, or *mempo*. Adorned with grotesque and fearsome features, such as arched eyebrows and a scowling mouth, the mempo not only protected the samurai and helped to keep his helmet secure, but it also served to frighten the enemy. The helmet, too, was decorated with intricate and fantastical designs such as horns, dragons, or other creatures. These designs were supposed to strike fear into opponents; they also identified the warrior and his family. Most helmets featured a small hole at the top to provide both ventilation and a place for the samurai's topknot.

Japanese armor was lighter than the bulky armor worn by **medieval** European knights. This allowed for ease of movement, especially in the hand-to-hand combat favored by samurai. The lightweight uniform also provided more comfort in Japan's sometimes warm weather, but it wasn't always effective in protecting a samurai against heavy blows.

WITHOUT A DAIMYO'S SUPPORT, SAMURAI WOULD NOT HAVE BEEN ABLE TO OUTFIT THEMSELVES PROPERLY

Samurai armies needed supplies, such as food, while stationed on battlefronts both near and far from home. The daimyo was responsible for gathering and transporting the supplies needed to feed his samurai and horses. Because Japan's hilly terrain was not suitable for wheeled transport, daimyo often required samurai and animals to form supply chains on foot. Samurai carefully protected these vulnerable supply lines, for if supplies ran out, battles had to be cut short. At times, rather than trying to transport the great number of supplies needed, daimyo ordered their samurai to take over villages, where peasants were forced to give them food.

READY FOR ATTACK

Samurai fought on two fronts: the fort and the battlefield. Samurai commonly traveled to an enemy fort or castle and laid **siege** to it. Early forts were made of wood and were therefore particularly vulnerable to fire. To attack stone castles, armies would try to break down walls or **catapult** large stones over the walls. A samurai army usually tried to cut off the food or water supply to a fort, which often ended in the fort's surrender.

On the battlefield, opposing samurai armies lined up across from one another, each samurai astride his horse. Then the samurai charged, firing arrows while galloping toward their opponents. This required great skill. A Chinese invention, **stirrups**, allowed a fighter to stand up while riding a horse. Once the opposing armies got close enough for hand-to-hand combat, the

fighters dismounted their horses and challenged one another to individual swordfights.

In the 13th century, the samurai fighting style changed after the Japanese suffered two attacks from Mongol invaders. The Mongols (a people from mainland Asia) fought in highly organized groups and outnumbered the Japanese, nearly defeating them the first time. In the second battle, a typhoon blew in from the sea, eliminating the Mongol enemy and saving the Japanese from defeat. The Japanese called this typhoon the kamikaze, or "divine wind." After the Mongol invasion, the samurai realized that they needed organized armies and coordinated attacks in order to be strong in war. They recognized that their bow-and-arrow tactics no longer guaranteed success. As a result, samurai became

EARLY SAMURAI FOUGHT ON HORSEBACK (OPPOSITE); 20TH-CENTURY KAMIKAZE PILOTS DROPPED BOMBS (ABOVE)

more dependent upon their swords and spears in battle. Instead of firing arrows from a long range, samurai warriors rode close to their enemy on horseback to inflict serious injury or death with the sword.

Samurai fighting style changed again in the 16th century with the introduction of the European musket. The Japanese admired this gun and adapted it for use in their battles. A few years after the gun's introduction into Japanese society, samurai armies were relying heavily upon the weapon, and soon Japanese gunsmiths were producing large quantities of firearms.

Whether relying on bows, swords, or guns, samurai armies looked to their daimyo as the head of their army. The daimyo controlled most aspects of warfare: he decided the plan of attack, who would fight, and who would stay behind to defend his property. Daimyo generally accompanied their samurai to battle, but they stayed at the back of the battlefield to give orders, protected by a large number of body-guards, as a daimyo's death in battle would cause a huge loss of morale for his samurai army.

The daimyo's orders filtered down to a second layer of samurai leadership. A daimyo's

The samurai fighting style lives on today in the martial art of kendo, which means "way of the sword." Girls and boys in Japan practice kendo in gym class, and kendo tournaments are held around the world. Participants use a bamboo sword and strike one of four parts of an opponent's body—the top of the head, the wrist, the ribs, or the throat, scoring points for each hit. Fighters wear armor to protect themselves. Matches are lively, swift, and loud, but—unlike in a samurai battle—everyone leaves with his or her life and limbs intact.

relatives—sons, grandsons, brothers-in-law, uncles—or trusted advisors held secondary leadership positions and were called *hatamoto* (officers). The officers in turn ruled over samurai called *go-kenin* (loyal followers). Sometimes samurai recruited peasants, called *ashigaru*, to fight in their army for a limited time. A samurai's rank within the army usually was based on how much land he controlled. If he was able to obtain more land through war or marriage, he might move up in rank.

Samurai training started early, when boys from samurai families were around seven years old. They studied closely with samurai and learned valuable subjects such as reading and writing. They also started to train in martial arts and played games that emphasized quick thinking and strategy. A young samurai studied under a more experienced samurai. The bond between teacher and student ran deep and was called *shudo*, or *bido*. Shudo was very important, as it was the way samurai tradition was passed down from one generation to the next. The devotion the samurai teacher and student expressed for each other was nearly as deep as the loyalty they

EVEN WITHOUT SAMURAI, MANY JAPANESE CHILDREN CONTINUE LEARNING THE WAY OF THE SWORD TODAY

expressed to their daimyo masters.

A samurai teacher might come upon his young charge at the most unexpected moments and surprise him with the strike of a stick. This taught the hopeful warrior that he must always be on guard. When practicing weaponry, the focus was on perfect form. Young students first practiced with wooden sticks. Using weapons was more than a physical pursuit; students also learned to focus their minds on the task. Between the ages of 12 and 18, students took part in a coming-of-age ceremony called *genbuku*, in which they received their sword, said goodbye to their family, and chose a new name.

Samurai trained not only in physical skills but also in psychological skills. The mind of a samurai required toughness and mental **agility**, which he worked to develop throughout his life. To do this, the samurai spent time in quiet contemplation, thinking about death. He used techniques of **Zen** discipline to quiet his mind and control his fears. This taught him to be rational and use his mind, for if he acted unreasonably in war and made rash decisions,

the results could be disastrous. Great dishonor fell upon the samurai who faced certain defeat on the battlefield. In this case, many samurai chose to commit suicide rather than meet shame, capture, or inevitable loss.

A samurai's suicide was particularly gruesome. The preferred method of taking his own life was to slice his belly. This action, known as seppuku (or hara-kiri), was first noted in the 12th century. Samurai believed that their spirits resided within their stomachs, and killing themselves in this manner was thought to be the quickest way to die. Eventually, seppuku came to be seen as a brave way to die and was reserved only for samurai.

Over time, the seppuku ritual evolved and became quite elaborate. The samurai, clad in white, knelt upon a white cushion. He grasped a sword and brought it to his belly, then cut lengthwise, from left to right. A close friend stood behind him—his job was to cut the samurai's head off to lessen the samurai's suffering. Although samurai who were defeated in battle often chose to commit suicide of their own

LIFE FOR THE JAPANESE IN THE TIME OF THE SAMURAI WAS DIFFICULT AND SOMETIMES BLEAK

The samurai obsession with death is easier to understand after one takes a closer look at the conditions in which samurai lived. They, along with all the people of Japan, faced hardship on a daily basis. Natural disasters such as earthquakes, floods, and torrential rains wiped out crops and farm animals, and often resulted in human death. Without a food supply, the people faced famine regularly. No one understood disease or how the human body worked, so illness frequently claimed young lives. Because they saw death all around, samurai grew to appreciate the fleeting beauty of life.

accord, others were forced to kill themselves as punishment for a crime. Some samurai chose to commit suicide if their lord died in battle. Samurai might also perform seppuku to persuade a lord to change his ways if all other negotiations had failed.

A samurai who failed in battle or failed to protect his daimyo was a dishonored samurai. If he didn't commit ritual suicide, the failed samurai roamed the land and became a beggar, looked down upon by all. He had lost his honor and respect. Without them, he was no longer considered a samurai.

A SAMURAI COMMITTING SEPPUKU

THE BRAVEST AND THE BEST

Successful samurai warriors were noted for their courage and bravery and earned an honored place in society. They were like today's rock stars or professional athletes, revered by many. Tales of their exploits filtered down from generation to generation, and their legendary actions remain important stories in Japanese history and culture. Some of the earliest tales of legendary samurai stem from the 12th century, but the best-known are from Japan's later years.

One well-known samurai tale relates the story of Oda Nobunaga (1534–82), who rose to power at a time when chaos and **anarchy** ruled Japan. At the time, the country was split into a number of small factions, each ruled by powerful daimyo who were constantly at war with each other. Nobunaga was born to a minor lord who was always fighting to gain land and power. Nobunaga rose through the samurai army ranks, first by establishing control of his own warring family, then by controlling and defeating neighboring provinces. One of Nobunaga's first stunning victories came in 1560, when he defeated a rival clan in the battle of Okehazama despite the fact that his army of 5,000 was greatly outnumbered. Soon after, Nobunaga built himself into a powerful leader and warrior with one overarching goal: to unite Japan and become leader of the entire country.

In order to accomplish this, though, Nobunaga had to get rid of those who opposed him, including the country's Buddhist monks. Nobunaga was fascinated by Christianity and welcomed missionaries to the island. This fondness for Christianity put him at odds with the monks, who were powerful because peasants tended to identify with them. Afraid that the monks might lead an army against him, Nobunaga sought to eliminate them. In 1571, he

WESTERN TRADERS WERE RESENTED FOR THEIR ARROGANCE

Occasionally, brave individuals led rebellions against powerful daimyo and their samurai armies. One such individual was Amakusa Shiro (c. 1621–38). Born in the 17th century to a poor farmer, Shiro was a smart young man who read and wrote extensively. As a Christian, Shiro wasn't allowed to freely practice his religion, since daimyo thought Christianity represented Western interests. Seeking religious freedom, at the age of 16, Shiro led a rebellion of 37,000 people against the daimyo. The rebellion lasted four months, until all of the rebels, including Shiro, surrendered and were killed. Today, a statue of Shiro stands on the Japanese island of Kyushu.

and his army attacked a monastery at Mount Hiei, killing those who refused to surrender. Some historians believe that around 3,000 people—monks, nuns, and their family members—were killed that day.

Throughout his career, Nobunaga helped to change the way samurai fought. Guns had just been introduced by **Westerners**, and Nobunaga trained himself and others on how to best use them in battle. He also built strong stone fortresses that could withstand gunfire. Nobunaga was close to his goal of uniting the country when his two top generals, upset over the way he had been treating them, turned against him and killed him in 1582.

Unlike Nobunaga's generals, many samurai throughout history distinguished themselves by their loyalty to their daimyo. A legend of such loyalty has been handed down through history in the tale of the 47 *ronin*. Although the tale has become the basis for many fictional books and works of art, it began as a real-life story. The story begins in 1701, when a daimyo named Lord Asano (1667–1701) went to visit the shogun, Tokugawa Tsunayoshi (1646–1709). Also in attendance was another daimyo, Lord Kira (c. 1600s–1703), who insulted Asano. Angered, Asano lost his temper and, in a fit of rage, drew his sword and attempted to kill Kira. Because Kira was well-respected, tradition dictated that Asano commit seppuku. As a result, his samurai became ronin, or masterless samurai.

MANY JAPANESE TRANSFERRED THEIR LOYALTIES FROM THEIR DAIMYO (ABOVE) TO CHRISTIANITY (OPPOSITE)

mand of Japan's large national army, which attempted to wrestle control away from the shogun and place it back in the emperor's hands. In 1868, Takamori led the army to victory over the shogun in the Boshin War, leaving the emperor in control. Although he held an official post loyal to the emperor, Takamori disliked the West's influence over Japan. He also wanted to go to war with Korea—a country Japan was trying to wield influence over—because Korean officials failed to recognize Japan's emperor as head of state. Other leaders opposed the plan, and Takamori, disenchanted with the government's central power, resigned. However, he was well-respected, and a number of samurai followed him to his hometown, where he opened an academy for samurai training.

In 1877, Takamori and his followers revolted against the government because officials instituted a number of reforms unfavorable to samurai. For one, samurai were no longer allowed to carry their weapons. In addition, the government stopped the centuries-old practice of requiring farmers to provide rice **stipends** to the samurai. Takamori's revolt, called the Satsuma Rebellion, pitted his army against the imperial army. Although Takamori's samurai waged war against the imperial army for several months, the rebellion was ultimately unsuccessful. Takamori was badly injured in the final battle, and legend says that he committed seppuku. He's considered a great hero in Japanese history for revolting against the government and Western influence.

Although most samurai were male, sometimes female samurai fought alongside their warrior husbands. Just like men, if they fell into dishonor, they were expected to commit seppuku. One legendary female samurai was Tomoe Gozen (c. 1161–84), who served in the divisive Gempei War from 1180 to 1185. The war pitted two rival clans—the Minamoto and the Taira—against each other. Gozen led part of the Minamoto army and participated in battle as fully as any male samurai. Many women of this time could skillfully wield a spear, but Gozen was also skilled in the use of the bow and arrow. Known for her bravery, Gozen often completed dangerous scouting missions. She died on the battlefield, and her heroic death makes Gozen one of Japan's most endearing cultural figures to this day.

THE IMPOSING SAIGO TAKAMORI (OPPOSITE); THE BEAUTIFUL AND BRAVE TOMOE GOZEN (ABOVE)

THE END OF AN ERA

Before the samurai era formally ended in 1867, the need for such warriors had already been declining for a couple hundred years. Intense fighting took place between warring daimyo in the 15th and 16th centuries, but by the end of the 16th century, a number of important rulers managed to unite the country. For the next three centuries, Japan experienced a time of relative peace, and the need for the samurai's fighting ways lessened.

Samurai retained their importance as members of Japan's higher class; however, instead of fighting, many took jobs as **bureaucrats** for their daimyo. By the 18th and early 19th centuries, they carried their swords as a symbol of status but rarely needed to use them. They still held the power to kill anyone who disrespected them, but few appear to have taken advantage of this right. Samurai continued to live by the bushido code and heavily emphasized

values such as education and respect. If anything, samurai even more closely followed bushido since they spent little time fighting. They formalized the code and urged the rest of Japanese society to follow its principles. With their extra time, samurai also pursued roles as learned scholars.

The beginning of the end for the samurai can be traced to 1853. In July of that year, United States Navy Commodore Matthew Perry (1794–1858) guided four ships into the harbor at Edo (modern-day Tokyo). Perry led an American expedition to find out more about this mysterious island nation. Until this point, Japan had managed to stay mostly isolated from the rest of the world. The country engaged in only limited trade with the West, and shoguns closely controlled any contact with foreigners.

The U.S., however, wanted to open trade with Japan. Perry threatened to declare war against the country unless those in power agreed

PERRY'S ARRIVAL MARKED THE END OF THE SAMURAI'S ERA

to open its lands to outsiders. As Japanese officials looked out into the harbor at giant American ships with large guns and cannons at the ready, they saw no other choice than to agree to Perry's demands. Even their most powerful samurai warriors would be no match for the heavy ammunition. By 1854, Japan agreed to allow U.S. officials into the country to explore and trade.

The era of isolation had ended. The world was now connected in a complex global network. In order to compete in this new world, Japan decided it needed a larger, more forceful army to guard itself against possible attacks. This army needed powerful, modern weapons—not ancient swords and spears—to ensure success. Japan expanded its imperial army, drawing soldiers from all social classes. The samurai, with their suddenly old-fashioned weapons, were no longer in demand.

Samurai and daimyo rebelled against the government in the 1860s in an attempt to keep Western influence from infiltrating the country. Then, in 1868, Emperor Mutsuhito (1852–1912) restored order and claimed power, the first Japanese emperor in centuries to hold actual power. The way of life the Japanese had known for 700 years, with shoguns, daimyo, and samurai in control, suddenly ended. Samurai contin-

EMPEROR MUTSUHITO (ABOVE); JAPANESE ORIGAMI (OPPOSITE)

The Japanese are famous for their origami—elaborate designs crafted out of folded paper. Origami figures were made for many occasions, such as weddings and other celebrations. In the early days, the bark of the mulberry tree was used to make origami; this was expensive, so only the wealthy practiced the craft. Samurai warriors gave pieces of origami to each other as gifts, representing good luck symbols in times of battle. Sometimes samurai created origami boxes to hold valuable items. Over time, origami was formed out of paper, bringing the art to the masses.

ued to stage rebellions, with the last recorded rebellion being Saigo Takamori's unsuccessful Satsuma Rebellion of 1877. The remaining samurai class, no longer holding any power, retreated into the background and faded from the spotlight, becoming only a shadowy representation of Japan's past.

Although samurai disappeared from society, their ways have not been forgotten. The samurai's courage, honor, and bravery on the battlefield are character qualities that people of many cultures want to hear about and emulate. Unbelievable stories of suicide and war fascinate and capture attention. For hundreds of years, samurai have been immortalized in books and, in the last few decades, on the big screen.

In Japan, samurai tales remain popular. The television series *Mito Komon*, set in the 17th century, details the travels of a disguised samurai who hunts down criminals. He and his samurai companions dispense justice, and good triumphs over evil. The late Japanese film director Akira Kurosawa regularly featured samurai-themed work. His style and storytelling skills, embodied in such films as *The Seven Samurai*, are emulated by movie directors all over the world.

In Japanese literature, samurai take center stage in the 1980 book *The Samurai* by Shusako Endo. Based on a true story, the novel details the travels of samurai warriors who visit Mexico, accompanied by a Christian missionary priest. They reluctantly agree to convert to Christianity but face shame and persecution when they return home. Samurai remain central figures in Japanese comic books and **anime** series as well.

Samurai lore hasn't been popular only in Japan. The adventures of these fearless warriors also intrigue American audiences. The noted 1960 Hollywood film *The Magnificent Seven* is based upon the Japanese movie *The Seven Samurai*. George Lucas, creator of the *Star Wars* movies, even based his Jedi knights on samurai stories. More recently, Hollywood released the movie *The Last Samurai* in 2003, a story loosely based on the experiences of Saigo Takamori. Although the film takes some dramatic

A YOUNG *STAR WARS* FAN IMPERSONATING LUKE SKYWALKER, A JEDI KNIGHT IN THE MOLD OF THE SAMURAI

license—the fighting skills shown in the movie reflect samurai ways from the 16th century, not the 19th—it was a blockbuster. In books, American author James Clavell turned his avid interest in samurai into the 1975 novel *Shogun*, which explores the Japanese era when shoguns ruled the country, daimyo ruled their provinces, and samurai traveled and fought to defend their daimyo. The book sold 7 million copies in its first 5 years, and a 1980 television miniseries drew 130 million viewers.

Although samurai no longer exist, their fighting styles and philosophies figure centrally in the Japanese way of life today. Japanese kamikaze pilots during World War II flew their planes into enemy positions to inflict damage or death. The kamikaze looked to the samurai and their fearless perception of death for inspiration. In Japanese business, the bushido code followed so rigidly by samurai still rules. For example, workers in large companies respect and revere their leaders and pledge outstanding loyalty, just as samurai pledged loyalty to their daimyo.

Today, the flash of a sword, the cry of a warrior, or the solemn act of seppuku are nothing but fragments of the past. Samurai are symbolic of a time when Japanese daimyo wrestled each other for control of land and wealth, which resulted in violent, bloody battles. But samurai also symbolize a time of respect and honor. They've earned their place in history, and their influence is certain to reach many more generations.

TOSHIZO HIJIKATA (ABOVE), ONE OF THE LAST SAMURAI INVOLVED IN THE REBELLION AGAINST MUTSUHITO

A samurai's diet relied heavily on rice, which was eaten with every meal. Samurai added vegetables such as potatoes, radishes, cucumbers, and yams to the rice. They might also come across nuts and beans. Since Japan is an island nation, samurai ate large amounts of fish, and even octopus, jellyfish, clams, and seaweed. The religions of Buddhism and Shintoism usually prohibited the eating of red meat, so this did not become common in Japan until the 19th century. For drinks, sake, made of fermented rice, was popular. Otherwise, samurai drank tea.

GLOSSARY

agility—The ability to move with quickness and grace; being resourceful and adaptable either physically or mentally

anarchy—Having no government; lawlessness and political disorder typically rule the land during times of anarchy

anime—A type of Japanese animation that uses colorful graphics, vibrant characters, and action-filled plots, often set in the future

aristocratic—Having to do with a high social class that holds the power and privilege in some societies

bamboo—A tall, strong grass found in parts of Asia; some armor and weapons were made out of bamboo

breechcloth—A samurai's undergarments, usually made of cotton and tied together with string, over which he wore his armor

Buddhism—A religion of central and southern Asia based upon the teachings of Buddha, who lived around 500 B.C.; Buddhism stresses overcoming suffering by mental concentration and living in a moral way

bureaucrats—People who serve in a government marked by an adherence to fixed rules, formalities, and rigid authority

catapult—To throw an object over a wall or other barrier by use of a throwing mechanism that launches the object with great force

central government—A government, usually based in a capital city, that makes decisions for the whole country, instead of letting regional governments make their own laws

Confucianism—A religion based upon the teachings of Confucius, a Chinese scholar who lived around 500 B.C.; Confucianism is marked by living in a kindly way and respecting all people

forging—A process of working with iron through which the metal is melted and then hammered into a specific shape

matchlock rifle—An early gun and one of the first to use a trigger; when the trigger was pulled, a lit fuse made contact with gunpowder and caused the gun to fire

medieval—A person, place, or thing from the Middle Ages, the period of European history lasting from about A.D. 400 to 1500

morals—Principles of right and wrong, especially relating to the teaching of proper behavior and living through good conduct

ransacking—Searching thoroughly and often stealing some things, and in the process destroying almost everything in sight

Shintoism—The first religion practiced in Japan; Shintoism combines a love of nature with a worship of ancestor spirits

siege—To attack a fort or castle by surrounding it and threatening the people inside until they are forced to surrender

stipends—Regular payments, usually in the form of food or money, for services or to help defray expenses

stirrups—Footholds at the sides of a horse that facilitate ease in horseback riding

Westerners—People from the West, or the part of the world that includes the U.S. and Europe

Zen—A philosophy and sect of the Buddhist religion characterized by the seeking of enlightenment through quiet, meditative practices

INDEX

Cohen, Richard. *By the Sword: A History of Gladiators, Musketeers, Samurai, Swashbucklers, and Olympic Champions*. New York: Random House, 2002.

Macdonald, Fiona. *How to Be a Samurai Warrior*. Washington, D.C.: National Geographic, 2005.

The Metropolitan Museum of Art. "Arms and Armor Around the World: Japan." Knights in Central Park. http://www.metmuseum.org/explore/knights/japan_sam_1.html

Ribner, Susan, and Dr. Richard Chin. *The Martial Arts*. New York: Harper & Row, 1978.

Richardson, Hazel. *Life in Ancient Japan*. New York: Crabtree Publishing Company, 2005.

Shintaku, Melanie. "Tomoe Gozen: Female Samurai." BellaOnline: Japanese Culture. http://www.bellaonline.com/articles/art18012.asp

Seal, F. W. "Military Aspects of the Daimyo." The Samurai Archives. http://www.samurai-archives.com/military.html